CURSED

ON

A TREE

The Journey. The Spiritual Process. The Healing.

by

DR. ANDREA HILL

DR. ANDREA HILL

All editing and typesetting of this manuscript was orchestrated by:
Dr. Nes International Consulting & Publishing
P.O. Box 70167
Pasadena, CA 91117
www.drnesintl.com

Book Cover Design: Renaldo Wade, Fly Monster, LLC
Photo: AG Photography
Makeup: Face by Scotti

Contact the Author by email at dreahill7@gmail.com

ISBN: 9780999178584

DEDICATION

To my father, Andrew Hill, Jr. and the memory of my mother, Opril Hill: Thank you for a beautiful childhood and for instilling in me a love and firm belief in the word of God. I am who I am because of you and I am forever grateful.

My sisters and brothers who have always looked out for me, Elma, Crystal, Gary, Sebastian, and Todd (RIP Hirouth): I pray that the healing power of God will be your portion!

To my daughter, Mariah Christina: You are my greatest inspiration!

To my great niece and nephew Joshua Martin and Jurnee Martin: Auntie Peach loves you to life!

This book is also dedicated to that young girl or boy who may be browsing the web or through a bookstore for books and comes across Cursed on a Tree. I pray that there will be an eternal impartation of the truth of God's word in your life.

ACKNOWLEDGMENTS

My sincerest thank you to the Intercessors who stood in prayer with me. Pastor Shadrach D. Martin and Co-Pastor Tiffani L. Martin, for standing with me in my darkest hour and never leaving my side until you were certain that everything was all right. Your sacrifices will never be forgotten and will return to you a hundredfold! To my L!VE Church Family, I love you all dearly! Thank you to Bishop Elijah H. Hankerson, III and Lady Rachel Hankerson; Bishop Ronald Irving and Lady Deborah Irving; Pastor Gary L. Pleasant and Lady Karen J. Pleasant; Pastor Fred Andrews and Lady Juanita Andrews; Pastor Rose McFerren and Deacon Herbert McFerren; Pastor Anita Johnson; Mother T. Marie Brown; Mother Yvonne Martin; Mother Junetta Richardson; Brenda Sodamade; Dr. Tamara Otey; Jaqueline Harris; Valerie Like; and Dr. Aleta Johnson. Special thanks to Anita Martin, Marie Moore, Kenya Butler, Marquita Gandy, Lilnora Green, Crystel Conner, Michelle Evans and Robin Jaouni.

To those who went above and beyond the call of duty to make sure I was okay and had everything I needed! To my childhood best friends Inetta Warren and Lisa Cannon. To Antoine Allen for helping Mariah take care of me! To my aunts Marea Hutson, Joyce Garner, and Vannessa Reynolds. To my cousins Mrs Ina Faye Richie, Carolyn Jones, Sherrie Harris, Brenda Joy Gilmore, and Monique Bucannon.

To Michael Jones thank you for never allowing me to go to one doctor's appointment or taking one test throughout this process without praying for me first! Thank you for being there even when you were 3000 miles away.

Cursed on a Tree

To Monica Witherspoon for helping me to jumpstart this project!
To Sandra Thompson Williams, thank you for your guidance and assistance. I could not have completed this project without you!

To those who gave me the push I needed to complete this book: Pastor Linda White, Evangelist Latrice Ryan, Elder Leandra Green, and Prophet Carey Gidron.

To Pastor Marcus O. Mickles for your spiritual insight.

A heartfelt thank you to all of my family and friends; you know who you are, everyone who prayed, visited at the hospital and home, called, texted, sent a card, flowers, stuffed animals, balloons and gift baskets, who brought food to the house, offered to keep my home clean, clean my laundry—would have even walked the dog if I had one! I'm grateful for your love, concern and encouragement. You all were definitely a part of the healing process!

Thank you to the brilliant Dr. Hannah Ha and her staff. To the staff at St. Luke's West Hospital, for your kind hospitality.

To Dr. LaTasha Nesbitt aka Dr. Nes (of Dr. Nes International Consulting & Publishing)! You were an angel in disguise. Thank you for your consultancy and your expertise. You turned my vision of a book into a reality!

Lastly, but certainly not least: To the Greatest being in my life, who is my life. To the Bishop and Shepard of my soul. To the Bright and Morning Star. To the Root and Offspring of David. To the Alpha and Omega. To the one who promised me that joy would come in the morning. My Lord and Savior Jesus Christ! Without whom there would be no book to write. This book is written to convey that I am not ashamed of the gospel of Jesus Christ, for it is the power of God unto salvation, to everyone that believes. To God be the glory for all that He has done!

DR. ANDREA HILL

All blank pages are intentional

FOREWORD

Dr. Andrea Hill is one whom God has raised up to be a Prophetic Voice. Her teachings are prophetically inspired to men and women throughout the nation. When I learned that she was diagnosed with a terminal illness, I knew without a doubt that God would heal her body and that He had a greater plan. This book is a result of God's plan to teach people everywhere to confess God's word by faith and watch it manifest in due time. It has been a great honor and joy working alongside Dr. Hill as she serves under my leadership as the Executive Pastor of LIVE Church. In this book, she reveals the total healing power of God. Dr. Hill is a praiser, a worshiper, but most of all she is a praying woman. Through her prayers and sacrifices, God worked a miracle in her life. I believe this book was written in love and from the voice of God Himself to bring healing by faith to all who read it. We will continue to pray and watch God work in your life. May God bless you in this hour. We decree and declare the favor of the Lord on this book and in your Life. Proverbs 10:22 says, "The blessing of the LORD, it maketh rich, and he addeth no sorrow with it." GOD BLESS!!

Pastor Shadrach D. Martin

Administrative Assistant Shadrach D. Martin

Senior Pastor LIVE Church, COGIC

BOOK REVIEWS

"This book by Dr. Andrea Hill will serve as a guide for those diagnosed with terminal illness. It will show them how to arise from the valley of hopelessness when it is easy to give up. It is a fight to persist in hope. From personal experience, Dr. Hill will show you how to fight and overcome despair."

Bishop Elijah H. Hankerson III, Missouri Midwest Ecclesiastical Jurisdictional Prelate and President, St. Louis Metropolitan Clergy Coalition

"I am so proud of Dr. Andrea Hill and the accomplishment she has made on her journey from pain to praise and from ashes to glory. This manuscript will serve as an outstanding book to the Nations. My prayers are with her as she shares her practical wisdom with much love, restoration, and healing to the heart of developing people around the world for the Kingdom of God."

Dr. T. Marie Brown, Supervisor of Women, MMEJ and Renown Revivalist

"This book is a delight to read. God still heals, and Andrea's faith is the go-between for that healing power. Supernatural experiences should be the norm in the Christian's life and Andrea is living proof that we are connected and can receive what God has always provided. This book will be an encouragement to all who read it."

Dr. Conny Williams, Chair of Cohen Institute

8

TABLE OF CONTENTS

All blank pages are intentional

INTRODUCTION

I vividly remember beginning a corporate fast in January of 2016. It was the beginning of the year, and I was starting it off with 21 days of fasting and praying. I had really been seeking God for the previous three months and desired to hear from Him concerning His will for my life. Fasting had been a practice of mine for years. Near the end of every year, I would begin to ask the Holy Spirit for clarity of direction for the upcoming year. God had spoken to me in October of 2015, during my personal prayer time. He stated that His word should be the central focus of 2016, and that the Word should be meditated on day and night. Well, I thought the Word of God was already the central focus of my life, but apparently, there was another level of the Word that I did not quite understand. This would eventually prove to be true.

I remember feeling excited about the direction God was leading me in His Word. I've always had a deep love and appreciation for the Word of God, ever since I was a young child. My parents had different Bibles and biblical study books around the house when I was growing up, and I was always reading. Whenever I would go to the mall with my mother, I would make my way to the book store and find the religious section! One time, when I was around eight or nine years old, I asked my mother for money to purchase a book that caught my attention. While reading the book in the bookstore tears began to form in my eyes and I'm not even sure if I completely understood what I was reading. However, I bought the book and each time I would read the book at home I would get teary-eyed but it was not sadness it was a strong sense of comfort. I later learned the author was a well-known evangelist named Kathryn Kuhlman who operated in the healing ministry. To this day, I do not remember what I read in the book; I only recall the fact that each time I read it, I would find myself wiping away tears. I have the same reaction today when I read books of or Flisten to recordings of Mother Estella Boyd, Mother Elsie Shaw, Rev. Kenneth E. Hagin and Bishop C. H. Mason. Even though these people are deceased, God's anointing was so strong upon their lives that it still resonates today through their audio and written works. There were times as a child that I would walk around with my Bible in my hands and I would be content.

I recall while in elementary school that our school's counselor was a Pastor. One of my friends and I asked our counselor if we could have Bible study at school during break time. I'm not sure how we pulled this off since prayers had been removed from public schools many years prior, but we led a campaign for Bible study, and it was allowed on a voluntary basis. I remember recruiting other kids to attend. The counselor eventually quit his job with St. Louis Public Schools and went into full time Pastoral Ministry. Since this meant we could no longer have Bible study at the school, we asked if he could take us to his church so we could continue this program. As a result, one Friday each month he would charter a school bus to come to our neighborhood, and there would be 20 or more youths who would attend the Bible study at his church. Those Friday night youth Bible studies were fun, exciting, and enlightening.

Since my love for God's Word was imparted at a young age, His instructions to go deeper in His Word in 2016 truly gave me a sense of excitement—it could only mean deeper depths, higher heights, and new revelations! I did not know all the details and really was not concerned about them, but I did know that God had a plan and a purpose. I was willing to follow that plan and that purpose.   I was confident in the fact that God had the details; he would reveal them to me in time.

In April of 2016 things began to change. One day after Sunday service, my sister Crystal offered to take me out to eat for my birthday which was the previous week. I accepted and the two of us went to brunch. Although we had a nice time, that evening I began to feel ill. I remember thinking to myself that the food may have been spoiled. I did not know if it was food poisoning, but I could not hold the food on my stomach. The next day I just felt sluggish and once again, I considered it was food poisoning. After that incident, I resolved within myself that I would not go back to that restaurant for a long time, if ever. And so, I let it go. Prior to this, I had gone on another fast in March of 2016; this one was a 15-day fast for the month of March. I also went on another fast that June. The latter fasts were corporate fasts with my church. I remember thinking that this was unusual: normally as a church, we went on 21-day "Daniel Fast" at the start of the year, at the request of my Pastor. Although it is always voluntary, most of the church members would comply. However, two fasts back to back was a little unusual for Pastor Martin to request corporately. But I do remember him saying he felt the Lord was leading the church each time. I strongly believe in fasting and praying.

I noticed near the end of the summer that I had lost quite a bit of weight. Since I have a small frame, six or seven pounds is significant. I remember thinking, "I'm losing weight because of all the fasting." I was not new to fasting, so going on a 21-day fast or 15-day fast was not unusual. So, I noticed the weight loss, but after the fast was over I knew I would go back to eating, and I generally regained my weight pretty quickly. I remember observing my weight loss and thinking to myself, "I probably have not really given my body time to gain the weight back." I felt like it would return gradually. As time progressed, the weight did not come back. In fact, I began to lose more weight. I scheduled an appointment with my primary doctor that October.

The visit went well. My doctor did not notice anything physically wrong from the examination I was given. When I returned for another doctor's visit, I had lost a total of nine pounds. My doctor still did not notice anything to cause alarm. Nothing in the physical exam made her think anything was wrong. I did advise her that I had some digestive issues that had been causing me some concern, even though I did not think it was anything major because it was only bothering me every now and then. Near the end of the appointment, I took it upon myself to ask her if she thought it would be in my best interest to have a colonoscopy. I had never had one before, so I know that it was the leading of the Lord for me to suggest this procedure. She said, "Sure why not? Let's get one scheduled for you."

I made an appointment and had the colonoscopy scheduled for November. Due to a scheduling conflict, the appointment was rescheduled for December. Before I could have my colonoscopy, I made an appointment with my primary doctor because I was still losing weight. One night early that December, I was in bed about to fall asleep. I was thirsty, so I got up to get a drink of water. As I entered the kitchen, I sensed a strong but sweet and soothing presence that caught my attention. I have felt this presence several times before down through the years; it was the presence of God. As I turned to look around, not expecting to see anyone or anything, I uttered, "Praise God, thank You Holy Spirit." I turned back towards the kitchen and heard a still voice within me say, "Peach, you're all right." I knew in that moment that it was the Holy Spirit speaking to my heart, but the voice was clearly my mother's voice. It was the same reassuring tone she would use when trying to encourage and assure me that things were going to be okay and that nothing was wrong. Peace came upon me.

Throughout my crisis, I would often think back to that day standing in the entry way to my kitchen, hearing my mother's voice assuring me that all was well. I would resort to the same peace that I felt that day. Peaches is the nickname my father gave me as a baby, and most close friends and family still refer to me as Peach, Peachie or Peaches to this day! My mother, however, would always call me by the name Peach. There's nothing more comforting than a mother's love and wisdom in a time of crisis. Little did I know that I was about to embark on the fight of my life, for my life. I began to praise and worship God because I knew that it was God's way of telling me that everything was going to be all right!

Friends, please understand that this was in no way a communication with my deceased mother. In no way was this necromancy, in any form. I did not have nor did I seek to have a conversation with my deceased mother. I've been told that when a person is learning to hear God's voice, that voice will often sound the same as the voice of the individual's mother or another trusted figure in the person's life. I was very familiar with hearing God's voice speak to my spirit man, but now I was in a situation where I would have to hear God as I had never heard Him before. My life literally depended on it. And he used my mother's reassuring voice to remind me that everything was going to be just fine. It kept my faith anchored throughout this process. This was God's way of comforting me because God sees all and He knows all – and He knew what I was about to endure.

I made an appointment with a particular doctor; I advised him that I was coming because I felt like I had lost more weight than was healthy. At this point I needed an explanation for the weight loss, so he fit me in for December 16th. This doctor ordered an ultrasound and other tests, including blood tests and stool cultures. Later, I got a call informing me that all the tests came back normal. I underwent a colonoscopy on December 19th.

I remember that day very vividly. My sister had a friend who had recently undergone the procedure, so she was able to discuss the prep procedure with me. She told me what I would have to drink and that I could not eat any food. I was looking forward to getting this whole thing over with. The next morning my sister and my father accompanied me to the appointment. I remember that my sister and I sat there and talked and talked and talked, anticipating them calling me back. Finally, they called me back. I remember waking up with a nurse standing over me, telling me that the doctor would come and speak with me. My sister was sitting right by my side when I woke up. Shortly afterward, the doctor came in and spoke: "Ms. Hill, unfortunately in your colonoscopy we did see a mass on your colon. And I do believe that this mass is cancerous."

I was stunned as I lay there. I was not expecting that. I was not even looking for that. The last thing I was looking for was cancer! The doctor went on: "What we are going to do is send the biopsy off for a pathology test, and that will confirm whether it is, in fact, cancer." She added, "In my experience, with what I see on your colon, I do believe that it is cancer. When the pathology report comes back, your primary doctor will instruct you further."

After hearing that, I just remember lying there calmly. I'll never forget the nurse who was in the room as well. She came back in after the doctor left, and she extended her apologies and began to encourage me. "You know you're young," she said. "You're still very young. You can fight this." They were pretty much convinced before any other testing had been done. Both the nurse and the doctor were sure that this was cancer.

The three of them (my sister, my father, and the nurse) began to encourage me and reassure me that everything was going to be ok and that they were praying. Soon, my sister and dad went to get the car. After I got dressed, the nurse grabbed my hand as she walked me to the car. I'll never forget this: she not only grabbed my hand, but she kind of wrapped her arm around mine and held my hand with one hand. With her other hand, she began to caress my hand in a reassuring way. And as we walked to the door she said "You're going to get through this," and she never stopped caressing my hand. "You're going to get through this. You're going to get through this," she kept repeating. When we got to the door she said, "I'm praying for you." And I knew that's what she was doing the whole time she was walking and rubbing my hand. I'm a believer. I know the power. I know the transference of laying hands, and I do believe I sensed it.

When we got to the door, someone she knew was standing near it. I could tell there was somewhat of a personal relationship between them, because that person asked her about an individual and her response was, "Oh that person was at church. I saw that person at church yesterday." And so, I knew she was praying.

During the ride home, I was still trying to internalize the whole thing. Cancer. Life had just changed for me. And more than likely, it would never go back to being the way it was before the moment I received that devastating news. I was blindsided.

1

NOT THEN, NOT NOW

As we drove I continued to wrap my mind around this whole thing. My father asked if I needed anything from the grocery store. It was not far away, and I said yes. When we arrived, I realized that I could not get out of the car and walk through the grocery store. I just could not because of the weight of the news I had just received. I could not do it. "I do not want to go in," I said to my dad and sister. "I cannot go in the grocery store." So, my sister and my father went in for me, after I told them what I wanted. But as they got out of the car and closed the door, I could hear my sister sobbing. She broke down crying. I did not turn around to look. I heard it. I knew what it was, because tears had begun to roll down my cheeks as well. Before they even got out of the car, the tears began to roll down my cheeks.

I sat in the car trying to wrap my mind around the news I had just received. I then started thinking about things that I had planned for the upcoming months. I was going to start a new position on my job in a few weeks. I had a list of things that I had to do the first of January; this included work for the church, classes that I had agreed to teach, and events that I had to plan. With this new challenge before me, I began the test of my life. I knew I had to make some adjustments.

One of the first things I did was to call my Pastor and First Lady to ask them to pray. Next, I called my best friends, Pastor Gary and Lady Karen Pleasant. I informed them that nothing had been confirmed but the doctors believed I had cancer. As I was giving them this news, I heard Lady Pleasant begin to sob and cry. Pastor Pleasant began to reassure me; I remember clearly that from the very start, his responses were all assurances. "God's got you," he reminded me. Then he reminded me of a sermon I had preached at their church several months earlier. In that sermon, I had given a testimony of the words that my mother had given me about finding out she was pregnant with me. She did not want any more kids at that point, because she had already had four babies back to back. She had been pregnant five years in a row, so there was little distance between the children. By the time she got pregnant with me, she did not want any more children. Overwhelmed at the thought of being pregnant again, she set out to have an abortion. Pastor Pleasant reminded me that she'd tried to have an abortion, but she could not do it. My mother did not drive. She told me that she'd asked one of my uncles to take her to some "back alley" place that she was informed about. This place was not a medical facility but some place that was known for performing abortion off the record. My uncle promised he would take her but could never find the time. Other rides never came through for her either. Finally, my Father convinced her to stop trying and assured her that bringing another child into the world would not be a hardship on the family. The abortion that my mother was seeking never happened! My mother said she eventually settled with the fact that she was having another baby. She told me that when she gave birth, her hospital roommates and nurses were asking if this was her first child because she could not stop hugging and kissing her new baby girl! She would tell everyone that asked, "No I have four more at home!" I made my entrance into the world, praise God. Pastor Pleasant reminded me that I'd brought that word to their church. He said, "You know the devil wanted to take you out then! He wanted to end your life before you were born. But he could not do it then, and he cannot do it now. You're going to get through this. You shall live and not die". And I believed it. That comparison gave me what I needed to fight. He (the devil) could not do it then, and years later he was trying it in another manner – but he wouldn't prevail. Thus, began the journey of my fight of faith.

As I began to pray that night when I went to bed, I shed tears over the thought that I may have cancer. One reassuring scripture that came to me was Proverbs 18:10: "The name of the LORD is a strong tower: the righteous runneth into it and is safe." That scripture was rhema to me in that very moment. "Rhema" means a portion of scripture that is illuminated by the Holy Spirit to bring life application to a situation. This verse spoke to my heart, it became alive to me. They were not just words written in the Bible; they were powerful, life-saving words. I really needed them, because as I called on the name of Jesus I found refuge, peace, and safety from the horrible, devastating report that I had received earlier that day. Within that Rhema moment, my faith was increased, and my total trust was placed in God. I got up out of my bed, and I stood in my bedroom, and I began to cry out, "Lord Jesus I thank you because I am safe." I felt certainty and assurance about one particular thing: I am the righteousness of God in Christ Jesus. This is not my own righteousness, which is as filthy rags (Isaiah 64:6). But Christ's righteousness has been applied to me, according to Philippians 3:9. Since I am the righteousness of God in Christ, this gives me access to run into His name. In the name of Jesus, I'm safe. There was no doubt in my mind about that. I began to repeat it: "I am the righteousness of

God in Christ Jesus. This gives me access to run into His name, and I am safe." Glory to God! Glory to God!

Reflections
Questions

1. Recall a time in your life when you received bad news. How did you handle it?

2. How do you find God's peace?

3. How have you provided comfort to others in the times of chaos?

Reflections

Reflections

2

I'M SAFE

E arly the next morning I received a call from my niece, Tiffani. It had to be about 6 a.m. that Tuesday morning. Tiffani gave me a number and asked me to please get on a prayer conference call. The prayer call was *The Awakening Prayer Call*, hosted by Evangelist Latrice Ryan. During that call, the woman of God began to pray. Something she said shot through my spirit with great force: "God's going to do it for His name's sake. God says my name is on the line. My name is on the line. And because His name is on the line, He's going to do it for his name sake." And that was enough for me to hear. 1 Samuel 12:22 says, "For the LORD will not forsake his people for his great name's sake: because it hath pleased the

LORD to make you his people." I felt as though God did not waste any time giving me encouraging words. He wasted no time imparting His word and encouraging me for the battle to come. He caught me before I even got out of bed that morning, before I could even start thinking on the news I had received the day before—before depression and discouragement could settle in my mind.

I continued praying and believing God. I was waiting for the pathology report to come back. The report should have come by Wednesday, but I did not get it until Thursday. My primary doctor called to inform me that the report confirmed that the tumor was cancerous. "It is cancer. I'm so sorry, but it is cancer," she repeated. I was stunned. I sat there in silence while she continued to talk. This was not the news that I was praying to receive. I felt as though the world stopped. The only other time I'd felt this way was when my mother passed away as I held her hand. The doctor began to give me some medical terminology for the tumor that I would not remember. But she told me what I needed to do next: "We want you to have a CAT scan. I'm going to order more blood work. And we want to set up an appointment for you to see a specialist. But we want you to have a CAT scan and the blood work before you actually see the specialist. The specialist will need to view this information. I want you to see a colorectal surgeon."

I did not want to tell my family and friends right away. I did not want to give them the bad news, because everyone was praying and believing for a different report. When I got off the phone I began to sob. That was not the news I wanted to receive. It was not the news I believed I would receive. But the news was given. All I could do in that moment was cry. Once again God wasted no time, because He spoke into my spirit immediately. "It's not over. It's just a process. It's not over," is what the Spirit of God spoke as I sobbed and paced the hallway in my home.

I did not want to call my family, but I did call Michael who was in California working at the time. I knew I could trust him not to tell anyone the recent news. Michael had been calling me every day. Two or three times a day he was asking me if they had called with the results from the pathology report yet. I did not want to discuss it with others, but I did call to tell him the results. "You know, we're going to get through this. We're going to get through this. We're going to pray. And we're going to get through this. You're going to be all right," he told me. And he prayed. I did not say much I just listened, still stunned. But he would just repeat those words to me. Besides my mother, I think he is one of the most optimistic people I know.

Reflections

Questions

1. Consider a time you believed God, but His will was different than you own.

2. When things don't go according to plan, what's your natural response?

3. Name three people that you can call during a crisis.

Reflections

_____

_____

_____

_____

_____

_____

_____

_____

_____

_____

_____

_____

_____

_____

_____

_____

_____

_____

Reflections

_____

_____

_____

_____

_____

_____

_____

_____

_____

_____

_____

_____

_____

_____

_____

_____

_____

_____

3

THE BLOOD STILL WORKS

After talking to Michael, I decided it was time to inform my employer. I was scheduled to start a new position beginning in January, and I knew at this point it would not be wise to start a new position with the diagnostic testing and doctor's appointments that I was facing. I called my supervisor and informed her of the pathology report that resulted in cancer. When I told her, I remember silence for a few seconds, and then she responded. "Andrea, you already know what to do." She began to remind me of a situation she went through years prior and how I encouraged her to pray and believe God. She was very encouraging and supportive and told me not to worry about the new position and that she would take care of that situation.

After that, I found myself pacing the floor again and saying "Lord, I trust you" over and over until I made my way to my daughter's empty bedroom and sat on the side of her bed crying. I was struggling to hold on to my faith. I felt as though I was in a mental battle, wrestling with giving in to the news that I'd just received or trusting solely in God's word for healing. It got to a point where all I could say was, "Jesus!" I was crying and screaming loudly in an attempt to drown out the doubt, unbelief, and defeat. I got up from the bed and began to make my way down the steps still screaming to Jesus. At that point, saying that name as loud as I could was my only anchor. It was the thing that held me together in those crucial moments after receiving the devastating news. As I reached the bottom of the stairs, I made my way to the living room area, and I remember collapsing on the floor between the couch and ottoman. I laid there still crying and calling out to Jesus. Soon I felt a strong presence of God, as though I was engulfed. The presence had a calming effect even though I was still crying. I no longer felt as though I was wrestling with my thoughts and feelings. It was peace. I was reminded of a day several months prior, when I was in church on a Sunday morning. There was a high worship in our service, and I remember my pastor, Pastor Shadrach Martin, standing and declaring the blood of Jesus, repeatedly. It seemed as if he repeated this a hundred times or more. Lying there collapsed on my living room floor reminded me of how I had collapsed at the altar that Sunday. My pastor was still declaring the blood of Jesus. I lay there several minutes with tears flowing and could not move. It was as though I was arrested in the presence of God. There I was, having just received a cancer diagnosis and I found myself in that same bodily position, at home weeping in the presence of God. God spoke to my heart in that moment and said, "I knew that day when you were on the floor in church weeping in worship—I knew that day what was in your body. My blood was shed for this cause." I continued to lie on the floor in my living room, still weeping, but also listening to the voice of God. There was such a peace that came upon me, and as God was speaking I began to hear the lyrics of a hymn in my spirit. I began to sing it with tears still flowing—but I was singing, "Blessed assurance, Jesus is mine, oh what a foretaste of glory divine. Heir of salvation, purchased by God, born of His Spirit, washed in His blood." At this point I felt refuge, comfort, and strength.

As I continued to lie there, God began to give me instructions on how to apply the blood that Jesus shed by way of his crucifixion for my circumstances. He told me to pray and confess. I was to speak to my body. I was to make a demand on my body to conform to what God's word says concerning healing from sickness and disease. That night I began to write down my confessions of faith. I began reaffirming my faith and beliefs about divine healing. The Lord even instructed me to have specific individuals to pray with me, so I assembled a team of intercessors. Actually, God had assembled this team of intercessors long before I even received this diagnosis of cancer. This was huge because I am a very private person. I'm not one to really solicit prayers for myself. Usually if there was a crisis, I would stand and believe God alone, except for perhaps one or two individuals whom I would ask to stand in prayer with me depending on the situation.

Do not get me wrong, I'm not attempting to be super spiritual; that has just been my experience. But I also knew that God has others praying for us in situations even when we are unaware of their prayers! We may think we are praying alone, but the Holy Spirit will move upon the hearts of others and have them praying you through a situation, and you may never be aware of the fact that someone else was praying for you as well. God is awesome like that! I'm not against the prayers of other believers. Ironically, I preached a sermon at my church weeks before the colonoscopy titled, "Prayers of the Righteous." I did not realize until later that I was really preaching to myself. Still, I waited several days before telling my family the news. It was December 23rd, and I did not want to put a damper on anyone's holiday.

Reflections

Questions

1. How often do you pray?

2. Do you have others who you confide in with prayer is necessary?

3. When situations happened to us, we often focus solely on ourselves. Recall the last time you rendered a self-less act despite pain you may have been experiencing.

Reflections

Reflections

DR. ANDREA HILL

🐚

4

SUNFLOWERS

My family knew that I had the appointment for the CAT scan and that I had to see the specialist a few days after. But I did not let them know about the pathology report until after Christmas. And they were good... No; actually they were not good. They were just ok by the time I gave them the news. But they were not going to lose hope. And so I to the CAT scan appointment. I had lab work on the same day. Tiffani went with me to the appointments. She knew that I loved sunflowers, so she met me there with a big bouquet of sunflowers. They are my favorite flower because they are so bright and sunny. They remind me of a bright, sunshiny day. And I love those kinds of days. We were still praying and believing God....

We sat there longer than normal for the appointment. I was told at the registration desk that they had not received the approval from the insurance company for me to have the CAT scan. So that process took about an hour and a half; I was determined that I was not going to leave that appointment without having the CAT scan. I was very adamant with the receptionist that the whole approval process was not my fault, and if they needed an approval and did not have it, I should have been informed before I got to the appointment. So they started the process of trying to obtain the approval right away.

I sat there waiting, looking at my beautiful sunflowers, which was very comforting. What's interesting to me about sunflowers is that they undergo a unique maturing process. When they are young and still growing, at a certain point of the day they will gradually turn to face the sun. In this hour of my life I was just like that young sunflower, only I turned to face the SON. My face was fixed on Jesus and there was no turning away. He was my only hope. I'd put my total trust in Him.

Finally, the insurance company sent through their approval, and everything was set to move forward with the test. I remember the radiology technician coming to get me for the appointment. She said, "I just really hope there is a possibility that the scan would not show anything, and everything will be well." I smiled and said, "Yes that's my hope as well. I'm hoping there's nothing there and everything will be well too." After the CAT scan was done, she walked me out and said, "Hopefully I will not see you back here again!" "Hopefully," I answered. I was still believing God that every test that I took would some way, somehow come out negative. I did not want the tumor showing up on the CAT scan. I wanted to believe the blood work would show normal blood levels and would not show any signs of cancer.

Reflections
Questions

1. What external things bring you joy?

2. Describe when the last time your patience was tested.

3. What can you do to improve this patient test next time?

Reflections

Reflections

5

DO YOU GO TO CHURCH?

S o that was on January 3rd. I had an appointment with the colorectal surgeon on the 6th of January. I continued to make my daily confessions of faith. I continued praying and believing God. Some of my family members wanted to accompany me to the appointment to see the specialist for the first time. I was told this doctor would confirm whether the results of all the tests that I had taken were really cancer. I had a few family members with me that day. I felt as though I could have done this alone, but they wanted to be there. When we got to the appointment, I had my family to wait in the waiting area because I wanted to talk to the doctor alone first. The nurse kept coming in telling me that the doctor was on the phone. I am not certain if he was on the phone with my primary care doctor or the doctor that performed the colonoscopy, but he was consulting with another doctor concerning my results. I sat there probably for a half hour or 45 minutes. As I sat there, I just began to praise God. I just began to sing songs of praise:

You are great!
You do miracles so great!
There's no one else like you. No one else like you...[1]

I sang until the doctor finally came in and introduced himself. He was a nice man with a warm spirit and pleasant personality. He had the CAT scan results on the computer screen, and he asked if I wanted to see it. I immediately said no. I just did not have a desire to see it. And it was not because of fear or anything of that nature. I just did not want to look at it; I did not feel it was completely necessary for me to see. He would ask again before the appointment was over.

He asked if there were others who had come with me to the appointment and I told him yes, but I wanted to hear what he had to say alone first. The doctor confirmed all the results. Cancer was the diagnosis. He began to tell me the size of the tumor and the dimensions of the tumor. He went on to say that surgery was necessary. He said that he would

---

[1] Noel Richards is said to be the possible author. However, Juanita Bynum, Nathaniel Bassey, and Terry Macalmon recorded version of this tune as well.

want to take out about two feet of my colon, and he began to talk to me about everything involved. Before he got too far into the conversation, I stopped him. I think I just wanted to hear the official findings before my family came in. So, before he got too far into the prognosis I stopped him and asked if I could my family could come in. He agreed.

I brought my family into the office, so they could hear the doctor's explanation. Some of them started asking me, "Well, what did he say?" before we got in there! The doctor was so gracious that he started all over again. He began to explain to them what he saw on the CAT scan, what the course of treatment should be, and that he wanted to perform surgery to remove two feet of my colon. While he was explaining the surgery, he drew a picture of the colon to give me an idea of what was happening. He drew a circle around the colon to show where the tumor was located. My daughter asked him about chemotherapy. He looked at the CAT scan again and was nodding his head yes to chemotherapy. He said, "Looking at the lymph nodes on this CAT scan, I would want you to go into chemotherapy six weeks after the surgery." After chemo, he wanted me to go into radiation therapy. He also explained, "According to the blood work, the blood levels show signs that the cancer has metastasized," meaning the cancer showed signs of spreading through my body. He explained that this was why chemotherapy and radiation therapy would be needed.

I was still really just sitting there. My family was doing more talking than me. The doctor continued to explain the surgery and wanted to schedule it for January 25th. However, the surgery that he described meant taking out two feet of my colon, and that just did not set well with me. I thought to myself, "Why not just go in and take out the portion where the tumor is? I wondered if the other part of the colon could be reconnected to the remaining colon once the tumor was removed. That's what I was thinking. I'm not a surgeon; I knew absolutely nothing about colorectal surgery, nothing about colon cancer. But as the doctor was talking, I envisioned a different approach to removing the tumor. I was leery of him taking out a whole two feet of my colon, because I knew it was only five feet long. The doctor asked me if he could schedule for January 25th. "I have an opening for surgery on January 25th;" he said, "we can go ahead and get that scheduled today." I looked at him strangely, and he looked at me. "I can tell you want to have a second opinion," he said. And I said, "Yes, I do. I want to have a second opinion." I presented my case to him: I was not comfortable with the hospital where he worked. He informed me that this particular hospital was the only hospital where he worked. Since I already knew that I was not that comfortable being treated there, I dreaded the idea of having to be admitted there. The doctor began to suggest some different facilities. He listed the doctors he knew who were colorectal surgeons in different facilities. I made the decision to go home and do some research on doctors and facilities myself. He advised me to have another CAT scan. This time it would be an upper CAT scan of my lungs, just to make sure there was nothing there and that everything was clear. I took his advice and scheduled the second CAT scan. As I was sitting at the desk scheduling the CAT scan, my family and everyone had come out of the office. The doctor came out and tapped me on the shoulder and asked me to come back into his office. He said, "I want to do another exam. I want to examine your stomach and abdomen area." So, we went back into his office. Just as he was about to do the exam he asked a surprising question: "Do you attend church?" he asked. "Yes, I do attend church;" I answered, "Oh…you do not seem to be worried," he said. "Are you worried?" I told him that I was concerned, yes, but I also knew my trust was in God. I had put my total faith in Him regarding the matter. I said, "I may have a resolve about me because of the fact that my faith and my trust is in God". So, we began to talk. He asked me where my church was located and similar things; it was actually a good conversation. He also shared his church affiliation with me and we discovered we had a mutual acquaintance between my Pentecostal church and his Lutheran church. However, when I left his office I felt hopeful in everything he told me concerning the diagnosis. Unlike others, he did not come with the doom and gloom.

Reflections
Questions

1. Are you a Christian? If so, how long have you been one? If not, find a bible and follow the directions in Romans 10:9.

2. Do outsiders know you're Christian? Do you think it's important to for them to know this information?

3. Describe you church experience.

Reflections

Reflections

6

I'VE SEEN GOD DO SO MANY THINGS

When I left the doctor's office that day I went home and called some other family members to let them know about the cancer diagnosis. At this point I had been told by three doctors that I had cancer, so I began to inform some other family members about the situation. I called my cousin Ina Faye Richie. At the age of 83 my cousin is the matriarch of our extended family. My mother and grandmother have both gone home to be with Jesus. My cousin Ina Faye and my mother were very close from childhood. Cousin Faye is the 'go to' person in the family, and we are blessed that God still has her here to impart her Godly wisdom. My sister had been asking me since the colonoscopy if I had called Faye to tell her what I was going through, but I did not want to call her until after I had taken all the necessary tests and received the results. I know she is a praying woman. She's solid in her faith. I finally called and informed her about the cancer diagnosis. She really did not say much other than, "Hmmm…" She really did not have a response. I asked for her daughter Carolyn's telephone number. My cousin Carolyn also had colon cancer some years prior. Therefore, I wanted to inform her. When Carolyn went through her diagnosis and surgery she contacted me; she said she knew I would pray. So, for the very same reason, I wanted to contact her –I knew that she was a praying woman as well. Cousin Faye expressed concern with the news I gave her, but we did not talk long. She told me to call Carolyn right away. Before I could get off the phone with Faye, Carolyn clicked in on a 2-way call. I told Faye that Carolyn was calling me now, so I would have to hang up and take her call.

Carolyn and I talked, and I explained to her that I had been diagnosed with colon cancer. She was quite surprised by the news. I could tell that the news really did hit her hard. I could hear the disappointment in her voice. She began offering her services by saying whatever it was that I needed, she could do. She assured me that she would be right there. She inquired about my doctors; she asked me who I saw and where I went. She began to tell me about her doctor and the confidence she had in her. She said that her doctor had performed a groundbreaking surgery on her, and she highly recommended that I see the same doctor for my second opinion. She gave me her doctor's information and I agreed to call.

After I got off the phone with Carolyn, Ina Faye called me back. "Peach," she said, "you know when you told me you were diagnosed with colon cancer? I know I did not say a whole lot. I do not want you to think that I was dismissive or unconcerned," she said. "But I did not have a reaction because I know that I've seen God do so many things over the years, and cancer to God is like pulling a tooth. It's major to us; man says it's incurable, but to God nothing is too hard! I know He's going to heal you," she said. Her words gave me another charge of faith. I mean it really boosted my faith, and the words she spoke encouraged me. She spoke from her years of walking with God, her years of watching God make a way when there was no way possible, and her years of witnessing God perform miracles! Her words were faith-filled, and it strengthened me to believe even more that nothing is too hard for God. Absolutely nothing. Yes—when you hear the word cancer, it seems insurmountable, and we know that cancer is an incurable disease. But there is nothing too hard for God. Nothing is irreversible with God. So, from there I was strengthened, I was encouraged, and this built my faith up even more.

Reflections
Questions

1. Experience allows us to maintain faith in God. Recall times when God performed an answer to your prayer.

2. Do you pray regularly or only when a problem arises?

3. In what ways can you make adjustments to your prayer life?

Reflections

Reflections

7

WHAT IF?

I did not call the doctor's office that day. I called the following Monday to schedule an appointment. I was told that the doctor was booked up for about a month or so and that she could not see me. I explained that I was calling for a second opinion appointment but unfortunately, she was booked and there was little to be done about it. I was disappointed, but I did leave my name and number in case an appointment came up sooner. After I got off the phone, I called Carolyn back and let her know that the doctor was booked up for about a month so she would not be able to see me. I told her that I was going to possibly start looking for another colorectal surgeon. Carolyn and I talked a long while about it. She kept reassuring me that she was going to be right there with me.

I did not call another doctor right away. I did go back to my insurance company and started searching for surgeons. I went through a list of colorectal surgeons in the area, and searched for doctors affiliated in hospitals where I would not mind being admitted if I had an inpatient stay. Yet I still had not called anyone to schedule an appointment. But that Thursday, I got a call from the same doctor's office; she could see me on Tuesday. They gave me a list of items they would need. "We need your CAT scan report and blood work, and the doctor wants any test you've had done this year in 2017," the receptionist said. "She wants to see all that information along with the colonoscopy report." Needless to say, I was very pleased that she could see me that Tuesday. I got off the phone and I called Carolyn. I said, "Carolyn, guess what? Your doctor's office just called and said she can see me Tuesday!" "I know," Carolyn said, "I've been calling that office every day since you told me they could not see you right away. I called and told them that you needed to be seen now. I let them know that this is a second opinion visit and you do not have a whole month to wait or longer." Thankfully, she was able to help get an appointment very quickly.

So that Friday I got off work early. I began to go gather all the necessary information. I went to the hospital where I had the colonoscopy, CAT scan, and blood work. Some of the information was sent to the specialist's office. I had some of it released to my hand directly, so that I could give it directly to the doctor when I went for the appointment. When Tuesday came, my cousin Carolyn went to the appointment went with me. I was very pleased with this doctor. She had a pleasant personality, and she made it easy to sit down at her desk and talk with her. We even made small talk concerning shoes! She's a shoe lover like me, and she showed me her stash of shoes in her office! Then she explained to me that after looking at the CAT scan and going over the test results, what she saw was cancer. Then she began to describe the type of surgery that she had in mind. I had not discussed anything about the type of surgery that the other doctor wanted to do. As a matter of fact, we did not discuss my first appointment at all. I just told her I was there for a second opinion. Not only did she describe the type of surgery that she would want to do, but she drew a picture of a colon to show me where the tumor was. She said she wanted to go into a certain area to take out the portion of my colon where the tumor is located. She said she would remove that portion only and take the end of my colon and reconnect it. "I'll reconnect your colon, and I'll feel up and down your colon to see if I feel anything else there," she explained. Her description of the surgery was actually what I had envisioned.

But she also said that if anything went wrong, or if there was leakage, she would have to go back the next day and perform another surgery; at that point I would have to wear a colostomy bag. No one wants to hear that; no one wants to hear that there's a possibility that they may have to wear a bag. But for some reason, I never even considered that I would have to wear a colostomy bag.

I felt more comfortable with her approach to the surgery. I felt more at ease with what she wanted to do to remove the tumor. I felt that if I had to have this surgery, it was better than taking out two feet of my colon. The doctor planned to remove only the part where the tumor was located. She also informed me that during the surgery she would look around my body to see if the cancer had spread to any other organs. If it had, I would need to see another specialist. She was very upfront and told me that if anything went wrong during the surgery, there was a possibility that I would have to wear a colostomy bag for life. I sat there, and tears began to roll down my face. The weight of the situation began to rest upon me. I became overwhelmed with the "what if's." What if these things went wrong? What if the cancer had spread? What if my colon leaked during surgery? What if I had to wear a colostomy bag? What if I do not make it out of this surgery? Ironically, the latter seemed worst for some, but it was actually the least concern for me. Because there's one thing that of which I am assured: whether sick in my body or well, this world is not my home. My life is hid in Christ.

When you are forced to come face to face with cancer, you come face to face with death. For the first time in my life I had to consider dying, but because my life is already hidden with Christ in God, meaning I have already accepted Jesus Christ as my Lord and Savior, then I have assurance that physical death of the body is not the end of it all. In Christ my spirit man has eternal life. Some people call it making peace with God. Jesus took the sting out of death, so it was not an antagonizing thought. 1 Corinthians 15:19 says, "If in this life only we have hope in Christ, we are of all men most miserable." Now let's be clear. I'm not saying that I wanted to die because the truth is that I did not, but it is not the worst thing that can happen to a Believer! As a Believer, a Christian, a Saved person, we know that our spirit man yearns for the New Jerusalem, New Heaven, and New Earth. This is according to Revelation chapter 21. We are living to live again.

The doctor told me that after the surgery, she would discuss the details of chemotherapy. But overall, I felt at ease. I did not feel uncomfortable. I did not feel as though 'this is not the doctor that I would want performing surgery on me' if I needed to have surgery. I was even pleased with the hospital where she worked. Afterwards, I sat down with one of her nurses, and she described everything that would happen the day of the surgery. We also went over some dates for the surgery. I informed her that before I scheduled everything, I wanted to go home to check with my insurance company. Since I work for an insurance company, I know the nightmares that come about if you are seen by a doctor or facility that is not contracted with your insurance carrier. I know the price that you can pay. So I told the nurse that I was going to go home and make sure everything was good with my insurance company. If so I would give her a call back so that we could schedule a date. And I did just that. I went home that day and discovered that everything was good with the insurance company as it pertained to this doctor and the hospital facility. The next day I called the doctor's office to schedule the appointment for surgery. The date selected was almost three weeks out, which made it February 7th. I was somewhat relieved that this was squared away.

Reflections

Questions

1. When was the last time you sought a second option with one of your life's challenges?

2. How often do you trust your instinct (or the still small voice)?

3. Recall a time when you did (trust you instinct).

Reflections

Reflections

DR. ANDREA HILL

8

MY CONFESSIONS

I began to inform my family and friends that I was scheduled to have surgery on February 7th. From that day to the surgery date I began to lose more and more weight. My doctor and I discussed the weight loss and she informed me that it was because of the tumor. She compared the tumor to a baby; everything that I ate, the tumor was sucking it up first. It was taking all the nutrients out of everything I ate, which is why I was losing weight. My concern was that I had not lost my appetite; I was still eating normally. My appetite was healthy, but I could not retain any weight and it was because of the tumor. She assured me that once the tumor was removed, I would gain the weight back.

In the meantime, the journey continued to unfold. I was still speaking my confessions every day throughout the day. I did it consistently. I had created for myself a rigorous regimen of confessing God's word over my body and declaring it to be true in my body daily. I recorded my confessions on my phone—if I was cooking or cleaning my home, I would play the recording or have my healing scriptures playing over the sound system throughout my home. I spoke to my organs, and I spoke to my colon. I spoke to my blood and my bones. I spoke to the marrow. I spoke to my pancreas. I spoke to my immune system. I spoke to my liver and kidneys and every organ. There was not an organ in my body that I did not speak to every single day. I made a demand on my body to align with the word of God. I was just speaking the Word of God so much so until it was as if I became one with the Word. That is the only way I can describe what I began to feel within me. I felt like every organ in my body had become the Word of God. Again, the Word of God that I was confessing over my body became Rhema, became alive, illuminating in my mind, body, and spirit. I believed that what I was speaking had taken place in my body. Hebrews 11:1 says, "Now faith is the substance of things hoped for and the evidence of things not seen." The words I confessed became my reality, despite the fact that I still had symptoms of cancer and was still losing weight rapidly. I believed every word that was spoken each day. The Bible tells us in Romans 10:17 that "Faith comes by hearing and hearing the word of

God." At home I was my own preacher! Whenever I felt down in spirit, I would begin to confess the Word. I went on and on doing this every day. From the time I got up in the morning until I went to bed at night, I confessed. Going to bed at night I would have my confession that I had recorded on my phone. I would let it play while I was sleeping. I played my healing scriptures while I was asleep so that the Word of God could soak into my spirit. If I woke up in the middle of the night I would start the recording all over again. This was something that I pretty much had to do to maintain my faith. I continued doing this in order to believe that healing would take place in my body.

I never doubted that God is a healer. I do not believe there is a Christian who believes that God, Jehovah Rapha—the God who heals—does not have the ability to heal. But few believe that healing can and will be applied to their own body. We read and believed the miracles of healing that happened in the Old Testament. We believe that Jesus healed the sick in the New Testament. But today, we can also partake of that same healing power of God. I had to continue to make these confessions every single day. There were some moments that I felt I could no longer do this. But because I had these confessions going all day long, it just became a part of my everyday life. Just as I was breathing air, inhaling and exhaling, I was saying these confessions just that much. They were necessary for me to stay focused on the Word of God, stay focused on the hand of God, and stay focused on the fact that I believed that my body would be healed. So when those moments came where I would begin to feel somewhat discouraged by the idea that I had been told that I had cancer in my body, I relied on my confessions. Just the thought of the word cancer could bring about discouragement, but the fact that I had these confessions going all day long, every waking moment, was the answer to get me through. These confessions were a part of me. I was confessing more than I was eating and quoting scriptures more than I was eating, because it was just a part of me. So, when discouragement would set in, it would last for only a fleeting moment. *Discouragement did come, but it could not stay.* The very minute it would set in, I would not give a whole lot of thought or space to it. I would think WOW they're saying I have cancer in my body and this is an incurable disease, but at the same time Galatians 3:13 would spring up in my spirit: **"Christ has redeemed us from the curse of the law, being made a curse for us: for it is written that cursed is every man that hangs on the tree."** And the curse is described in Deuteronomy 28:64, where part of the curse includes sickness and disease —but it was cancelled in the book of Galatians! To redeem means to make an exchange for something, to pay the price for. When Jesus was crucified on the cross, he paid the price for the penalty of sin. This price should have been charged to our account, but he paid it with His own life and in His own body.

Sickness and disease is a part of the price of sin; the curse of sickness and disease came through sin. I've been redeemed from that curse. I've been redeemed. It's because Jesus Christ was made a curse for me. I believe this with every fiber of my being. I believe that He took the curse.

This is what I meditated on day and night: the fact that Jesus took the curse for me on the tree, according to Galatians. "I do not have the curse of cancer. Cancer cannot dominate my body. Cancer has to be uprooted. It must be plucked out. Cancer cannot dwell in my body." These were the confessions that I began to make daily. I began to speak to my bones and command my bones to line up with the Word of God. I commanded my bones. I made a demand on my body and a demand on my bones to produce good marrow. I demanded the marrow to produce pure blood. And I would speak these things every single day. I'd make a demand on my colon to reject cancer. I would make a demand on my liver and my kidneys, lungs, and pancreas. I demanded every organ in my body to reject cancer. In Jesus' name, I demanded it. I'd tell my body that cancer could not dominate it. Cancer would not dominate this body. In Jesus' name, it would not dominate.

Reflections

Questions

1. Maybe you don't have a physical tumor. What tumors are in your life that suck the nutrients from your life?

2. How long has this tumor being in existence? What would it take for the "tumor" to be removed from your life?

3. What would situations in your life need confessions? Find the scriptures that correspond with them and make it apart of your life.

Reflections

Reflections

9

A TURN AGAIN BLESSING

One day, I began to think about the fact that every single diagnostic test I had taken had returned positive for cancer—Stage 2 colon cancer. I became overwhelmed with the thought of having cancer. These thoughts came upon me suddenly one evening. As I was going to bed, I was lying there and thought, "You know what? This is too much. This is too much for me to fight. I cannot fight this." As I laid down to go to sleep I did not have my healing scriptures playing, as had become my normal bedtime routine. I began to lose strength that night, and I told myself whatever happened was just going to happen. I was just going to let it be. Whatever was going to come of this, I'd just have to go through it. And I remember having tears in my eyes as I came to this conclusion. As I drifted off to sleep, I began to feel this nudge on the left side of my arm. My body would jerk, and I would wake up for a few seconds and fall back asleep. It was as if someone was trying to awaken me. This happened about three times. The third time, I saw the silhouette of a woman. This was more of a vision. I saw a silhouette of my niece Tiffani, who is also my pastor's wife. I looked up and I heard the Lord speak to me and He said, "Do not be afraid; only believe." And then He began to remind me of the King Hezekiah in 2 Kings 20:1-5, when the prophet Isaiah went to Hezekiah and told Hezekiah that his sickness was unto death and to get his house in order because he was going to die. The next verse tells us that Hezekiah turned his face to the wall and he prayed. He sought the Lord. He reminded God of how he walked upright before Him, and He cried out to God in faith. Hezekiah cried out to God because he knew God had the power to heal his body. Regardless of the fact that Hezekiah's illness was supposed to be incurable, Hezekiah knew that God had the ability to touch his body and heal his body. And his prayer moved God. It moved God's hand. And this is what God said to me: "I'm going to give you a turn again blessing." And He reminded me of how, in that next verse, the bible says that before Isaiah could get out of the city, the Lord spoke to Isaiah and told him to turn again. Go back and tell Hezekiah that I heard his prayer. I've seen his tears and I am healing his body. And so the Lord spoke to me and said, "The same doctors who told you that you had cancer are going to have to turn around again and give you a different report." I began to praise and magnify the God of my salvation. I began to lift my hands and worship God as never before. My strength was renewed. I got up and began my confessions again with such conviction. I laid down again to fall asleep, but this time, praising God and with my healing scriptures playing, I peacefully drifted off to sleep.

The vision of my niece Tiffani returned while I was asleep. My niece and I share a special bond. I am the youngest of six brothers and sisters. I was around 13 years old when she was born, so it was like I finally had a real, live baby doll! I was super excited about my niece's arrival. My nephew Marco is the oldest grandchild and I was just as excited about his arrival a couple of years before Tiffani's. When his mom and dad brought him to my parent's home for the first time as a newborn I remember running to the door in excitement! But Tiffani was the first granddaughter, my first niece. As a kid, I had the latest baby dolls on the market every year. I loved to dress them, feed them, and comb their hair! When my sister was pregnant with Tiffani, I remember the whole family happily anticipating her arrival. Right before she was born, there was a TV commercial about a popular baby doll named Tippy Toes. My mother started referring to her soon-to-be-born granddaughter as Tippy Toes! I remember after she was born, my mother and father would play with her and sing the commercial's jingle. So as a baby her nickname was Tippy Toes, and we eventually shortened the name to Tip! My brothers and I were very protective of our niece. I babysat her often on weekends when she was a toddler. She hung out with me and my friends, and she would try to stay up late to watch movies or listen to music with us. I remember once we were all in my room listening to music, laughing and talking, playing with makeup, just having fun. One of my friends pointing to the floor said, "Look at Tiffani!" We all looked, and she was just lying on the floor fast asleep. At first I thought she was playing, acting silly as she always did, but she was in a deep sleep. We were literally on the floor laughing because she never wanted to go to sleep; she thought she would miss out on some action! But that night she could not hang!

Throughout her adolescent and teenage years God would impress upon me to intercede in prayer for her. I was always praying for her and all my nieces and nephews; most times they had no idea. God would prophetically show me potentially dangerous situations that she would happen upon, and there were times when I would call to warn her and advise her not to go certain places. Once I had a dream that she was going shopping to pick up specific items that I needed from the store. When she arrived at my door with the items, it was late at night and she had tears running down her cheeks and a look of despair on her face. I could see a man behind her, but I could only see the lower part of his body. I was devastated; it was as if the look on her face said everything. When I woke up from that dream I felt that same devastation that I felt in the dream. I immediately began to pray for her protection. A few days later I had not given the dream anymore thought, and I never told her about it. She worked at a store, and I had called her earlier that day asking her to bring me some items that I needed from the store. Later that evening she called asking again for the list of items I requested and said she would come by after work to bring the things I needed. After hanging up the phone, the Holy Spirit brought the dream back to my remembrance. When I began to think about the dream, the look on her face, and the devastation I felt, with no hesitation I called her and told her not to bring the items, and that I would stop by to get them the next day. The Holy Spirit instructed me to stop her because the dream was about to become a reality. She later informed me that the same night she was also going to go out with friends and was going to stop by my house to bring the items afterwards. But when I called to stop her from coming to my house, she changed her plans and went home. I believe whatever the devil had planned for her was interrupted! Now my niece is a grown woman, a pastor's wife, a mother, a successful entrepreneur and a strong prayer warrior! Just as I prayed earnestly for her over the years, she was now praying earnestly for me.

Reflections
Questions

1. Have you ever been given bad news and hoped that somehow the circumstances would change and you would receive a different report?

2. Is believing God by faith for a Turn Again (a different report) that simple for you? Describe your process.

3. When was a time when your faith was weak concerning a matter and someone else said or did something that strengthened your faith?

Reflections

Reflections

10

THE POWER OF PRAYER

That night I had become overwhelmed with the thought of this illness. I began to look ahead at what could happen, what might happen; I became so overwhelmed that I became weak. I began to get in that mindset where I wanted to give up. But I remember in the vision, I saw Tiffani nudging my shoulder. She was jerking me, telling me to "Get up, get up, get up!" And in that moment, I realized she had been praying and interceding the whole time. She had previously told me that after receiving the news of my diagnosis, she had created a space in her home where she was praying specifically for me. She had shut everything out and she was praying on my behalf. Through intercessory prayer, she was able to reach me in the spirit realm during my weakest moment. Some refer to intercessory prayer as 'standing in the gap' for another person. A gap may be created because of momentary weakness, the weight of a burden, a loss of faith, or unbelief that will cause a person to give up on what they are praying for. Sometimes we may just need that extra strength in our inner man that intercessors provide through prayer. However, I believe intercessors are necessary for even the strongest believer. We all have our moments of weaknesses in crucial times. In the moment that I had determined within myself that I was giving up, her prayers reached me. And so, I got up in that moment when the Lord spoke to me; I had renewed faith. I regained my strength. I resumed my confessions. I put my healing scriptures back on. When the Lord spoke that word to me that he was going to give me a turn-again blessing and he likened it to Hezekiah, I began to praise and magnify my God. I began to speak to my body all over again. I began to encourage myself and encourage my body again. I grabbed ahold of my healing again, even though the illness in my body was contrary. I began to walk by faith and not by sight again! Glory to God! There were moments that came in to discourage me, but they did not last. God would always strengthen me all over again.

This is why it is so important for intercessors to pray. The ministry of intercession is imperative in the body of Christ. I know that some people—even some Believers—will say that intercessory prayer is not necessary today and that Jesus was the only Intercessor. I say that Jesus was the greatest Intercessor on Earth, and He's still making intercession for us according to Romans 8:34. But there are also many believers who have the spirit of Christ, who are filled with the Holy Spirit, which enables us to carry out the will of God, to occupy until He comes back (Luke 19:13). In other words, we do the works that He did and in an even greater capacity. The Gospel entails more than just preaching the Word. We must also do the Word. So even if you do not want to call it intercessory prayer, just do not stop praying on someone else's behalf! When you're interceding for someone, you're going to God on their behalf. You stand in their stead. And it's almost as if you're taking on everything that they are feeling. You take it upon yourself, and in their weakest moment you can reach God on that person's behalf when that person cannot. And that's exactly what happened that night. That was the first night that I had resolved to give up. But it did not last, once again. Why? Because the prayers were going forth, the Word had already been spoken, the confessions were already out there. My own words of confessions were already in the atmosphere. And God said that His Word would not return unto Him void. It will not return void. I had so much word already spoken, already gone up before God. And the Word did not return unto Him void; I got back in the fight. I began to fight harder.

When you are making these confessions and you're standing on the Word of God, believing the Word of God—that is a fight. You're fighting against the foe. You're fighting against the obstacles. You're fighting against the sickness. You're fighting against the disease. You fight against trials. You fight against tribulations. You fight against depression. You fight against oppression. You fight against financial situations in your life. You fight against it all with the Word of God. Because the battlefield really is in the mind. The apostle Paul says in chapter 10 of 1st Corinthians that the "weapons of our warfare are not carnal, but they are mighty through God to the pulling down of strongholds, casting down imaginations, and pulling into captivity every thought to the obedience of Christ". So, the fight is in the mind. The battlefield is in the mind. And that's why we must constantly renew our mind with the Word of God. It is not a one and done deal. Renewing our minds by reading the Word of God must be a lifestyle. Because if we're trying to fight against weight of the cares of life with any other weapon, it will not work. The bible tells us in Hebrews 4:12, "For the Word of God is quick, and powerful, and sharper than any two-edged sword, piercing even to the dividing asunder of soul and spirit, and of joints and marrow, and is a discerner of the thoughts and intents of the heart." The Word of God is quick and powerful. It is our most treasured and most powerful weapon against the enemy. The thoughts, the intentions, the plans, and purpose of God—

they are all found in His word. Our praise gives us leverage in this battle, and so does our worship. But we have to know and use the Word.

In Matthew chapter 4, verses 1-11, Jesus fasted for 40 days and 40 nights. The bible says that the tempter (the devil) came before Him, tempting Him to go against God's word. But Jesus responded to the devil with the Word. Each time, the devil came before Him to convince Him to go against the Word of God. And each time, Jesus would respond to Satan with the Word of God which was already written. He said, "It is written." In Matthew 5:18, the bible tells us that "heaven and earth shall pass away but not one jot or tittle of the Word until all is fulfilled." If God spoke it, if He said it, He's going to make it good. My confessions were based on the Word of God. Not just on my own desires. Of course, I desired to be healed but that was not enough. My confessions had to be based on God's Word. I needed something sure. Something that spoke to my situation. Something that spoke to my body. And I found that in scriptures. I found in Deuteronomy 28:61 that sickness and disease was a curse of the law. But then I found in Galatians 3:13 that Christ has redeemed me from the curse of the law. So that gave me something to fight with. That Word became my weapon. Because Jesus was the one who hung on the tree. He hung on the cross. He took sickness and disease upon Him on the cross. He was made that curse for me. And that's what I stood on. That's what I believed. And that became my reality. Glory to God!

Reflections

Questions

1. Name some intercessor in and around your life. Are you one for someone else?

2. Aside from Sundays, how often do you study your bible?

3. What scriptures are you mediating on currently for something you might be going through?

DR. ANDREA HILL

Reflections

Reflections

DR. ANDREA HILL

11

NO MORE FEAR

I was raised in a Pentecostal church. I am unapologetically Pentecostal! As a child, I thought there were only three preachers in the world: Pastor R. J. Ward, Pastor Dwight McDaniels, and Pastor James A. Johnson. The three would later become Bishops and grow their churches to become three of the most prominent Pentecostal churches in St. Louis, Missouri. These were great gospel preachers. As a child, I understood the simplicity of the message of the Cross as preached and taught by these men. Their teachings, based on the Word of God, shaped my theology. As I grew older I understood that there were great gospel preachers all over the world! Of different nationalities, races, and color. I have been blessed to have learned truths of God's Word from men and women of different denominations, as well as non-denominational believers. I never let a denomination barrier hinder me from hearing God's Word. In my extensive studies, I've learned a great deal from teachers who were Baptist, Lutheran, Methodist, Presbyterian, and more. I even enjoyed listening to Mother Angelica's teachings! My mother used to say, "Eat the meat and not the bones." I found this saying to be of great wisdom, because to educate yourself you must understand that just because you may not agree with certain aspects, it does not discount those aspects that are agreeable. Eat the meat and not the bones. Thereby you learn and grow.

Pentecostalism rose to the forefront of religious experiences near the beginning of the 20th century. We believe in the death, burial, and resurrection of our Lord and Savior Jesus Christ. We believe in His ascension after His resurrection and that He is soon to return. Pentecost is the Greek word for the Jewish Feast of Weeks. It is the 50th day after Jesus Christ was resurrected from death when the Holy Spirit descended and indwelled the believers. Pentecostals hold fast to a firm belief of baptism in the Holy Spirit, which empowers the believer with the ability of speaking in an unknown tongue, a language unknown and unlearned to the believer according to the first and second chapters of Acts. Pentecostals also believe in divine healing among other spiritual gifts according to 1 Corinthians chapter 12. These are my beliefs.

The first surgery was scheduled for Tuesday, February 7th. The Sunday before, during worship service, my pastor asked me to come for prayer and he began to speak to me prophetically with a word of wisdom and a word of knowledge. 1 Corinthians chapter 12 outlines the nine spiritual gifts given by God through the Holy Spirit to the Believer. The gifts are given by divine inspiration to instruct, predict, edify, and reveal those things which we cannot comprehend with our natural intellect. The spiritual gifts give supernatural insight of what would otherwise be unknown to the natural mind. This is not to be confused with psychic abilities. The spiritual gifts work as the Holy Spirit wills, not at our own will. On this particular Sunday, my Pastor asked me to come before the congregation. He said to me, "God told me to tell Hill (which is my last name) not to be afraid to go to sleep. And tell Hill not to be afraid to eat," he said. God knew that I had apprehension concerning those two things. Going under the anesthesia is one of the things that bothered me. I also had concerns about eating, because I did not want to get sicker. At this time I still maintained a healthy appetite, but the tumor was affecting my digestive system. There were certain things I would not eat because I did not want to get sick. Therefore, when he began to speak, I knew it was a word from God because going under anesthesia was weighing heavily upon me, but I had not discussed it with anyone. He proceeded to pray a prayer of faith and healing. Pastor Martin also informed me of something else. He said the warmth that you feel will be the healing power of God at work in your body. Divine healing and the prayer of faith is not unusual or spooky to me, since I was born and raised Pentecostal. I have witnessed others miraculously healed by the power of God as a result of faith-filled prayer. Therefore, supernatural healing is not unusual in a Pentecostal church and not only Pentecostals but other reformations are also operating in the gifts of the Spirit! It is a demonstration of the Spirit of God. From that day, I no longer feared the anesthesia, and neither was I afraid to eat!

Reflections
Questions

1. Be honest. What is your greatest fear?

2. When was the last time you confronted it?

3. Have you ever received or witnessed someone give a prophetic word? Have you spoken prophetically yourself? Describe that experience.

Reflections

Reflections

DR. ANDREA HILL

12

HOT & COLD

My Aunt Marea called me on the telephone that Sunday night. She called weekly, sometimes two or three times a week to check on me and to encourage me. She told me that night that she loved me and that she was still praying for me. While talking to her, she noticed that I had a cold. "You know you really sound bad and congested," she said. "You need to call your doctor tomorrow because she may not want to do the surgery with you having a cold," she explained. That was something I never considered. I did not know, because I had never been hospitalized and had never undergone major surgery. 1 had not been in the hospital for anything other than childbirth, so I was not familiar with all these different things, and the thought never occurred to me that this cold could interfere with the surgery. My aunt advised me to contact my doctor in the morning to make her aware that I had a cold.

That next morning, I called my doctor's office and spoke with the clinical staff. The person I spoke to said, "I'm going to give the dr this information, and she's going to contact you." Approximately two hours had gone by when my doctor called back herself. After asking a few questions concerning the symptoms I was having, she told me her conclusion: "I'm going to make the call to say let's not do the surgery tomorrow," she said. "With you having a cold, there is a risk of developing pneumonia during the surgery. I do not want your body to have to recover from pneumonia and the surgery at the same time," she decided. I definitely agreed with her analysis. I was not going to force her to do the surgery when she felt it would not be in my best interest. So, we rescheduled the surgery for two weeks out, which would be the 21st of February. From that day forward, I had an unusual experience. I remembered that I had received the word from Pastor Martin that I would feel this warmth in my body. Every single day leading up to the 21st of February, I would get this hot feeling in my body. I would get so hot that it would wake me up at night. I would go from being extremely hot to feeling extremely cold. And this went on every day. So much so that I would ask my daughter, "Mariah, are you hot?" And she would say, "No Mom, I'm not hot. It's not hot in here." Then, I would come back and ask her, "Mariah, are you cold?" And she would say, "No ma'am, I'm not cold. It's just you, Mom." And this would go on every other day.

The Friday before the surgery, one of the ministers from my church sent me a text message, and in that text message she said, "I was praying this morning and the Lord showed me you, how you would get really, really hot and then really, really cold. And God said he was healing everything, every sickness and disease out of your body." I sat up in the bed when I read that, because I knew that was God speaking. I had not informed anyone of my fluctuating body temperatures. I did not even call my doctor's office about it. I did not think it was a big deal. It was a sensation that I was getting on and off throughout the day. When she said that, it hit my spirit that God was healing my body.

Reflections

Questions

1. Delays are a part of life. Describe you process of waiting for something major to transpire in your life.

2. When was the last time you had to make a major change?

3. How do you adapt to change?

Reflections

_____

_____

_____

_____

_____

_____

_____

_____

_____

_____

_____

_____

_____

_____

_____

_____

_____

_____

Reflections

_____

_____

_____

_____

_____

_____

_____

_____

_____

_____

_____

_____

_____

_____

_____

_____

13

WHATEVER HE SAYS TO YOU, DO IT!

The Monday before the surgery, I got several calls from different people wanting to pray with me before the surgery. I recall my sister Elma calling and others. One call was from Mother Yvonne Martin. She told me that she had been in prayer concerning me and that God instructed her to tell me not to let anyone touch my body from that moment until I went into surgery. "God told me to tell you this," she said, "because He has sanctioned your body for healing and His healing power is still at work in you. Do not let anyone touch you." When she gave me those instructions I did not quite understand the reasoning. But I thought about when Jesus performed a miracle and turned water into wine. Jesus went to the wedding that He was invited to and was informed that there was no wine. Mary (Jesus' mother) told the servants, "Whatever He says to you, do it." So, whatever instructions Jesus was going to give to bring this miracle about, it was important that they follow the instructions. The instruction that He gave them was to go and get water pots and fill them with water. This actually made no sense, because water was not what was needed. They needed wine. But Jesus told them to get the pots and fill them with water and he performed a miracle of turning water into wine. The instructions did not make sense. What if the servants had said, "We do not need water in these pots, we need wine? Wine is made of grapes, and it takes years for them to be processed just right! We're not going to fill pots of water; it's useless!" But Jesus gave specific instructions to go get the pots and fill them with water. Then he brought about the miracle. Friends, it is so important to follow God's instructions to the letter. Place your total faith in Him and you will be assured of a miracle. We must trust Him even when we do not understand. So, when she told me that, I remembered this passage in my head and my spirit. I know Mother Martin to be a Godly, sober, praying woman, and I had no reason to doubt that God had given these instructions. I was determined to obey the instructions, whatever the reason. It was not for me to figure out, and it was not for me to question. If He said, "Do not let anyone touch your body until you go into surgery," I had to obey. And I did just that. I did not let anyone touch me. I let no one lay their hands on me to pray. I obeyed what the Lord said to do. Glory to God! I'm so thankful for the very few praying men and women of God who connected with me through this healing process. Some did it by way of social media, and some personally. However, the connection was made, it was for a greater good. These were people who did not just talk Christianity, but they actually lived it and were given to prayer.

Reflections

Questions

1. On a scale of 1-10, with 10 being the strongest. How strong is your faith?

2. Describe the last time your faith was tested?

3. What major lessons have you learned when you face challenging circumstances?

Reflections

Reflections

14

VICTORY

The day of the surgery was a rainy day. By this time, I had lost more weight. I was down to 113 pounds from my normal 135, but I was full of prayer. I had received several calls the night before from different people wanting to pray with me, so I was full of encouragement and full of faith. Surgery was scheduled for 7 a.m., and I was asked to arrive at the hospital at 5 a.m. I was surrounded by the comfort of my family and a few friends who met me there. The staff at St. Luke's Hospital was the most hospitable staff I've ever encountered in a medical facility! As I was prepped for surgery, I really did not have any anxiety, not even concerning the anesthesia as I once had before. Before I was to go into the surgery waiting area, my niece Tiffani wanted to pray. So, she, my sister Crystal, and my daughter Mariah all gathered to pray.

Once I was in the surgery waiting area and had been placed in a bed, my dearest friend Karen Pleasant arrived and we laughed and talked for a few minutes. I remember her saying to me, "For someone about to have surgery, you sure look cute!" By this time, the anesthesiologist and my doctor had arrived. Lady Pleasant knew it was near time for me to be taken to the operating room, so she got a little quiet, and then she asked my doctor if we had time to pray. My doctor replied, "Of course," and she and anesthesiologist stayed in the room for the prayer. Not only did Karen pray for me, but she prayed for every single medical provider who would touch my body. She prayed a very powerful prayer. I was absolutely covered with prayer before going into surgery! I remember as I was being rolled into the operating room, I was quoting to myself a chant Pastor Martin started a while back that simply says, "He's a miracle worker." I remembered that a couple of weeks before the surgery, Pastor Travis Cox had advised me to go into the operating room saying, "It's already done"! I thank God that I was very calm and relaxed. I was reminded of the scripture in 1 Peter 5:7: "Casting all your cares, all your anxieties, all your worries, and all your concerns, once and for all on Him, for He cares about you with deepest affection, and watches over you very carefully." It was even surprising to me that I was not worried at all! I had an unintentional pleasant smile on my face each time one of the medical providers addressed me. Once they put the oxygen mask over my face and told me to count backwards from ten, the very next thing I remember is waking up to a smiling nurse. The surgery took about 2-3 hours. When I was awakened, immediately the nurse informed me that the surgery went very well! She said, "We are going to take you to your room where you have a whole fan club waiting for you!" I was still very groggy, but I was able to comprehend everything she was saying to me. Once I arrived on the floor to my room, I remember my Uncle Herb and Aunt Rose were the first to rush to my hospital bed before medical technicians were able to roll my bed into the room. Then other family members and friends were there to greet me as well. Everyone had an excited look on their face. I remember going in and out of consciousness, and different ones would come to my beside to plant a kiss, say a prayer, or hold my hand. I could faintly hear the chatter in the room. I could hear some giving updates over the phone to different family members and friends who called to check on my condition. I remember my cousin Carolyn asking the nurse where my morphine pump was; she was concerned about the pain level that I might have once the anesthesia wore off. But praises be to God Almighty, I never needed morphine! The pain level was controlled with Ibuprofen and Tylenol! I specifically remember hearing Tiffani on the phone with someone, and I opened my eyes the best I could to look. I noticed she was pacing the floor as she talked. Others were sitting around talking, but my attention was focused on Tiffani. She was telling someone on the phone that my doctor told the family that she removed the tumor, and the cancer was contained in the tumor—she did not see any spreading throughout my body. She also told the person on the phone that my doctor told them she had to give me a blood transfusion; I had lost so much blood that I had become anemic, and she did not see how I had been walking around with the strength I had. I heard her say that my doctor said she would have test results back on Friday, and she would come that day to discuss chemotherapy and radiation therapy treatments. Much of that night is a complete blur to me, but I remember that conversation Tiffani had on the phone.

As much as I wanted to ask questions about her conversation, I really did not have enough strength and could barely talk above a whisper. I remember hearing my sister Crystal talking nonstop! I heard her tell someone on the phone not to come to the hospital because I was not able to really respond and that I needed to rest. I had a private hospital room, so it could accommodate everyone. My daughter Mariah and my niece Tiffani stayed all night with me and took turns feeding me ice chips. They would rotate throughout the night. They stayed with me the first three of the five nights that I spent hospitalized. Any time I grunted or sighed they would rush to my bedside. My spiritual daughter, Kenya Butler, came to the hospital late that evening after everyone else from my "fan club" had gone home. Mariah was there with me, but Tiffani had gone home to get some things and was coming back. Pastor Martin had asked church members not to come to the hospital to visit because I needed rest. But my spiritual daughter Kenya Butler came anyway that night! I was happy she did. I was awake at this point and still very weak. The anesthesia had begun to wear off. I remember her walking in with flowers and a worried look on her face. She said, "I could not get anyone on the phone; neither Pastor Martin nor Lady Tiffany would answer their phones, so I got concerned and had to come to the hospital to see you for myself." I assured her that all was well.

When I woke the next day, I was more alert. I had slept on and off the night before, because nurses and technicians were in and out of my room all night. It was not until the following morning that I realized that I had tubes everywhere. I could not even get out of bed to walk. I had oxygen tubes through my nose; both arms had tubes running through them; my abdomen had another device coming from it; and both legs were, as I called it, shackled. I could not get out of bed. I recall looking around the room at Tiffani and Mariah, both asleep. I looked ahead at the whiteboard on the wall with my nurse and medical technician's info. I saw my medication info and near the bottom of that board I saw the word **VICTORY** in all caps! Once again God caught my mind before I could slip in a state of depression over the circumstances where I found myself in that hospital bed. I was reminded of the scripture 2 Corinthians 2:14, "Thanks be to God, who always gives us the victory in Christ, and opens the savor of the knowledge of Him by us in every place." This was one of the scriptures that was a part of my daily meditation. I quoted this scripture every day several times a day! Later in the morning I still could not talk above a whisper, but I mustered up enough strength to asked Tiffani who wrote the word "victory" on the whiteboard and she replied, "Momma Karen wrote it!" Momma Karen is Lady Karen Pleasant! I'm forever grateful for my sister/friend!

Reflections
Questions

1. Despite circumstances, what things to you do to remind you of God's power?

2. Who are you in God? Do you understand your spiritual gifts?

3. Who are you in a crowd? Are you the motivator, encourager, teacher, etc.? What makes your presence special?

DR. ANDREA HILL

Reflections

Reflections

DR. ANDREA HILL

15

HOW DID I GET HERE?

T he first day was really rough, seeing that I had very little strength. I could not eat anything still, only the ice chips. When my doctor came to my room, she informed me that the surgery went very well. She explained how she removed the tumor and reconnected my colon with no complications. For that I was grateful. She also explained that I was anemic, and that she had to give me a blood transfusion. I was not aware that I had become anemic; I showed no symptoms or missed the faintest symptom. She advised me that starting the next day she would upgrade my diet; still no solid foods but at least I could have broth and juice! She also explained that she would not have my test results back until Friday to determine the course of chemotherapy and radiation therapy. She advised me of the daily progress that I needed to make before she would discharge me. I was determined to make the progress and to do everything she said I needed to do. After my doctor left my room that morning, I noticed that I had something wrapped around me. I grabbed it to pull towards my face so that I could see it, and I discovered it was a prayer shawl. I inquired about it and Tiffani told me that as soon as I got out of surgery and was brought to my room, she had wrapped me in her prayer shawl. As the morning hours progressed, I regained more strength and became more aware of my surroundings. I noticed music was playing constantly, and it was the same song on repeat. I kept hearing the words of the song, "You are great, you do miracles so great, there is no one else like you!"

I thank God for Tiffani, Karen and all the others who were at the hospital praying, because they created an atmosphere of faith in my hospital room. There was no room for doubt and unbelief. The room was full of expectancy for God to do the miraculous. As the song played, I asked Mariah for my phone. I wanted to hear the healing confession that I had recorded of myself speaking into my phone. I wanted to hear the healing scriptures that I would listen to daily via YouTube. I began referring to the day that I was admitted as Day 1.

Day 2

I was able to get out of bed with assistance and sit in a chair for only a few minutes. I was able to sip broth. These were major accomplishments! I continued my healing confessions throughout the day. That evening, Karen came back to the hospital and even though I was still weak we laughed and talked as we always did! Laughing was a task and extremely painful. Karen kept apologizing for making me laugh. She came up with a remedy for me: "Let's placed this pillow on your stomach to ease the pain when you laugh!" It helped somewhat! That's what friends are for!

Day 3

Once again, I was able to sit in a chair —a little longer this time! My menu was upgraded to pudding and gelatin. My doctor informed me that she ordered physical therapy. I was excited about it, because I wanted to make the progress to go home. The challenge came when the physical therapist came to my room. I was unhooked from all the tubes but still attached to the IV stand. I had no idea that walking would be such a challenge. As the nurse helped me to get out of bed I saw the physical therapist with a walker and I began to wonder why they brought a walker to my room. Previously, I would go from the bed to the chair with my daughter's help which was challenging enough. This time they wanted me to walk a few steps outside my room. I never imagined that it would be so difficult! When I realized I really could not walk by myself, I began to feel sad. I tried not to cry, but when they brought the walker over to me and I began to walk with the physical therapist holding my IV stand with one hand and my arm with her other hand, it took me what seemed like forever just to make it to the doorway of my room. When I got to the door, tears began to stream down. Not only was I out of breath, but it took every muscle in my body just to make it from the bed to the doorway. The physical therapist tried to comfort me. "This is good enough; we do not have to walk any further today if you do not feel up to it," she said. As I stood there, I asked myself, "How did I get here?" How did I get to this place of having cancer, hospitalized, and unable do things that I would normally have no problem doing myself? Daily task like walking and feeding myself became arduous tasks. But with tears rolling down my cheeks I said, "But God I trust you." The Holy Spirit spoke to me once again and said, "Just go through the process." I told the physical therapist that I wanted to walk into the hall. So, we walked a few feet and turned around. I was determined to make progress. I did not want to turn back at the doorway because to me that meant defeat. As I made it back to my room, I could do nothing but lie down. I was exhausted and in pain. The nurse hooked me up again to all the devices I had. But the sadness was gone and I felt strengthened in my spirit.

Day 4

I was able to make more progress. By now, I was doing everything my doctored wanted me to do. I could get out of bed slowly but painfully on my own, make my way to the chair, and order my meals. I felt really encouraged. Different people came to the hospital throughout the week to pray for me, or they would call to pray. The visitors, balloons, flowers, and cards were all very encouraging. Everyone who came was extremely helpful and was willing to do anything they could to help.

Reflections
Questions

1. Support systems makes all the difference. Name your team?

2. Are you a support system for someone? If not, think of ways you can support someone going through a difficult time.

3. Do visit people who are hospitalized? This is something that Jesus instructed us to do.

4. How do you handle frustration?

Reflections

Reflections

16

HE'S A MIRACLE WORKER

Day five in the hospital was actually the fourth day after my surgery. This was a Friday. Tiffani asked me the night before to call her when my doctor made her rounds to my room so that she could hear what the doctor had to say. This was the day I would learn my course of chemotherapy and radiation therapy. I did what became my normal routine since being hospitalized. I probably slept on and off for a few hours. Mariah and Tiffani both went to work that morning. I made my way out of bed and to the chair. I called the nurse's station for fresh gowns and toiletries. I really wanted to wear my own gowns and pajamas while I was there. I had gone shopping in early February and bought brand new sleeping garments just for my hospital stay. But after my surgery I realized I would not be wearing those items. It was utterly impossible, considering my surgery was abdominal and due to all the tubes and devices that I had connected to my body. In addition, the nurses and technicians were constantly in and out of my room giving me shots, labs, and checking vitals. My own garments would not have been convenient. After the first day, I refused to let the nurse's assistants bathe me. It was a tedious process for me to bathe myself. However, once I was cognitive enough, I informed the nurse's station that I would bathe myself. As nice as they are, they still offered to assist me every day, but I politely declined and would only request clean garments and bathing items. It was not easy, but my independence encouraged me to do so. I sat in the chair and began to look at the menu to determine what broth I would order. As I sat there, before I could order the broth, my doctor walked in.

She walked in saying hello and immediately she said, "I have good news!" She went on to explain that she had all 27 lymph nodes tested and there was absolutely NO CANCER found in them! She went on to say, "This means you do not need chemotherapy, and you do not need radiation therapy." My hands immediately went up! The only thing that would come past my lips was Praise GOD! I said it over and over and my doctor even repeated it after me! Praise God! She gave me a copy of the report and gave instructions to her nurse to remove the devices and tubes that I was hooked up to. Everything was removed! I felt as though I walked from one zone into another. I honestly felt as though I had awakened from a bad dream. As weak as I was, I began to give God all the glory, all the honor, and all the praise! She told me that I would be discharged the next morning, because she was now upgrading my diet to full solid foods! She wanted me to digest solid food before she would discharge me. After she left I sat there in amazement. Thank you, Jesus!!! Every confession that I spoke had manifested. The Word of God was manifested! I called my father to give him the news. He was so happy, and he began to praise God as well! I called Mariah at work and she screamed in tears! Her co-workers took the phone from her asking what was wrong. What happened? So, I explained it to her and the co-worker rejoiced as well. Afterward, I called Tiffani and Crystal, and they both rejoiced! I called Karen to give her the news. I'll never forget that she immediately started crying and saying, "Lord, you are so faithful!" I shared the news with my cousin Carolyn. She also began crying.

"I asked the Lord not to allow you to go through chemo or radiation," she said. Carolyn personally had been through chemotherapy. Although God worked a miracle in her life as well, her path to healing was different from mine. Nevertheless, He's a Miracle Worker!

Everyone's path to healing is not the same but Jesus is the same yesterday, today, and forever more. We serve a mighty God who does things in His own timing and His own way. He does not change, and His word will never fail. I still had a long road ahead of me, but I had joy in my soul! I believed that I could face anything.

Afterward, I called a few people to inform them of the "Good News!" My phone began to ring. The first call I received was from Lady Rachel Hankerson. The first thing she said was, "District Missionary Hill, Praise the Lord! Praise the Lord! We serve a miracle working God!" I did not know if she was speaking by faith or if she already knew the report I had received just moments before she called. I agreed with her, and she said, "I heard the report!" She and Bishop Hankerson had already received the phone call of the "Good News." We both rejoiced! After I got off the phone with her, my door opened, and it was Kenya and her co-worker. They came through the door rejoicing with excitement! Kenya was holding her phone videoing as she came through the door. Her co-worker immediately said, "We just had to see with our own eyes what a miracle looks like!" The "Good News" was spreading faster than I had imagined. My hospital room was full of joy. We praised God and laughed, and laughed, and laughed! A nurse walked in my room and she said you girls are having so much fun! The same nurse told me that she was so happy for the report that I received. As the nurse began to unhook more devices, I felt as though I was the captive being set free. Later, the same day, the physical therapist came to take me for another walk. This time I was able to walk slowly step by step but without the walker. I was determined. Even though it was painful, and I had to stop every few steps and hold on to the wall, I kept walking to the therapy room. When we walked past the nurses' station, one nurse looked at me, and she had a huge smile on her face. "Aren't you so happy? I'm happy for you that you do not have to go through chemo or radiation!" she said. I smiled and uttered, "Glory to God!"

Finally, the therapist and I made it to the therapy room. She wanted to teach me how to walk up and down stair steps. Once we arrived, I had to sit down. I was exhausted. Another lady in the room with her therapist had a walker, and she looked at me and exclaimed very loudly, "Why doesn't she have a walker?" She spoke in a tone of indignation and resentment. I was in pain and too faint to even respond. My therapist looked at the lady with a strange look. The lady's therapist responded and said, "Everyone's recovery process is not the same." I can still hear that lady's tone of voice today. My heart went out to her, because I knew she was dealing with the same emotions that I was dealing with the first day I tried to walk. I realized I could not do it alone. I needed the help of the walker. Only I did not become resentful or envious of anyone else who was in a better place than I was at that moment. I began to pray for her recovery and pray that she would call unto Jehovah Rapha! For He is the Lord that heals.

You may be going through an illness or know someone who is currently going through one. The recovery process may have resulted differently than mine. But it does not change the fact that God is still God. Jesus is Christ the Healer. God's abilities do not change based on our personal experience or circumstances. Regardless of the outcome, He's still God. I understood how this woman felt because it also reminded me of when my mother was in the hospital, and the doctors told us that she would not live through the night. While we were at her bedside praying, I had to leave the room to escort some other family members to her room. As I walked down the hallway I walked passed another room and I noticed the person sitting up in his bed and his visitors were laughing and talking with him. I immediately felt resentment. As I continued to walk I said, "God why can't we laugh and talk with my mother?" Why are we watching her slowly slip away?" I began to cry. God did not respond. After I had my moment, I began to realize that I was allowing bitterness to set in and I began to repent. I asked God to forgive me and began to thank God for that person's life and for that individual being well enough to entertain his visitors. That night my mom went home to be with the Lord! Later that evening God spoke to me and said, "While you were envious of what was happening in someone else's room because of their laughter, you did not realize that what was happening in your mother's room was precious in my sight." Precious in the sight of the Lord is the death of his saints (Psalm 116:15). God is still God!

The next couple of days after my good news from the doctor, my room were filled with more visitors, and everyone who came to the hospital came rejoicing in God. I was especially happy to see the relief in my father's countenance. Suddenly I was back to eating regular food and anticipating going home. I was not actually discharged until the following Monday. Tiffani and Crystal came to take me home. I had so much joy and peace and there was no doubt that God had done exactly what He promised me that He would do. The prayers and every confession spoken were not in vain. Upon discharge my doctor explained that I should schedule a follow up appointment with her within two weeks. She also recommended I see an oncologist to determine if the specialist felt a need to monitor my blood count. She stated that six months from my discharge she wanted me to have more blood work done and another colonoscopy. I also was to see my primary doctor. For necessary reasons, the remainder of the year was filled with doctor's office visits. With every visit that I had, each doctor marveled at the fact that I did not need chemo or radiation. Each one marveled at my recovery. I did not hesitate to let each one know that

Jesus is a healer! By June, I had begun to gain my weight back. I saw the oncologist and he was amazed as well. He actually told me that I had no need to continue to follow up with him. The oncologist explained the different tests that were run on the tumor that was in my body. He said they found no rhyme or reason for it. He said it was not even hereditary. He described it as some "fluke thing that happened." He said to me, "Whatever you are doing, keep doing it because it's working!" He implied that he was keeping his fingers crossed. I said it was prayer and faith in God!

After several doctor appointments, I finally had the colonoscopy near the end of the year.

Prior to the colonoscopy, my doctor ordered more blood work. It was October of 2017. I was back to my normal weight, back to work, and living and enjoying my life. I was scheduled for the follow up colonoscopy. Two weeks before the appointment, I began to feel a little apprehensive. My mind began to wonder if there's a tumor there again. The smallest abdominal pain would be magnified in my mind. I began to fight this battle in my mind and remind myself of what God had already said and what He had already done. I was healed in Jesus' name, and I kept reminding myself of this fact when I would have those moments of fear. When I arrived at the appointment at the same facility where I had the first one, it was all too familiar. I was back in the same place where I had received the most devastating news of my life. As I was being prepped for the procedure, I was still speaking God's word over my life to calm my nerves. I suddenly had to go to the restroom, and within me I began to praise and worship God. As I was about to walk out, the Lord God spoke to me and said, "Remember that night when you felt like giving up and I promised you a 'turn-again" blessing, likening the blessing to King Hezekiah? This was when Isaiah told Hezekiah to get his house in order because his sickness was unto death. However, after Hezekiah's prayer, I told Isaiah to turn again and tell Hezekiah that I heard his prayer and that he was healed of his illness." I replied, "Yes, Lord." The Holy Spirit said, "Now here you are in the same facility and the same doctor that gave you the bad report on December 19, 2016 is about to give you My Report." With tears streaming down my face I replied again, "Yes, Lord." The heaviness lifted. I wiped my face of the tears before I exited the restroom. My emotional strength was restored, and my spirit was renewed with that word from God. And just as the Lord spoke it, it happened. Up until this point I had not considered the fact that this was the same doctor performing my colonoscopy. The very same doctor that awakened me on December 19, 2016 to apologetically inform me that what she saw in my body was cancerous tumor, awakened me on October 21, 2017 to inform me that there was no tumor, and no polyps whatsoever. And this time she had a smile on her face! Glory to God! Hallelujah! I was hoping to encounter the same nurse who assisted me when I got the bad report. I believe in my heart that she was a praying woman. I'll never forget her walking me out to the waiting area and holding my hand. I knew this woman was praying. She said, "You will get through this; I'm praying for you." Her words were very comforting, but it was not what she said to me. It was the way she gripped my hand with hers, and how she used the other hand to gently pat my same hand. And she held my hand for a while. I'm a praying woman myself, and I'm an intercessor, so her actions and words were all too familiar to me. Praying people have the ability to pray the most effectual, fervent prayers and no one around us has to know that we are praying. But those prayers will prevail. We can pray boisterous prayers or silent prayers. However, it is our faith in God that causes our prayers to be effective. I did not see this particular nurse that day, but her prayers prevailed in my life. Not long after the good report of the colonoscopy procedure, I received even more good news. The blood work results came back completely normal! Hallelujah! Hallelujah! Glory to God in the Highest!

Reflections

Questions

1. Do you understand process? Write your own definition below.

2. What purpose does "process" have in the lives of believers?

3. Describe a current process you are experiencing. How are you handling it?

Reflections

Reflections

DR. ANDREA HILL

17

AS ONE WHO DREAMED

T hroughout this experience, my life was not the same, and I knew it would never be the same again. Somehow through this experience my life was very much enhanced. It changed me in many ways and gave me a whole new perspective. I understood the value of certain things and situations that I did not consider before. I now have more compassion than I once did for people deal -ing with chronic illnesses, because now I understand what it feels like to receive devastating news from a doctor.

Not that I was callous towards others before, but now I know the emotions that one will go through wondering should I just die and not even try to fight this. I have compassion towards those who do not know how to fight a giant such as cancer or any other insurmountable issue that life may bring.

I pray that this book will arm you with the mightiest weapon known to mankind, which is the Word of God.

Friends, the Bible is truth, and it is infallible. I understand what the writer meant in Psalm 126:1, after the people of God had been living in Babylonian slavery and captivity for 70 years. Suddenly, God changed the heart of the Babylonian king, and he set them free to return to their homeland. They were set free from slavery and the captivity of their oppressor. The writer said, "When the Lord turned again the captivity of Zion we were like them that dreamed." To go through one phase of being told I have cancer and seeing the effects of it on my body, to being told 65 days later that there is no cancer is marvelous. This was especially amazing because I watched my body bounce back as if nothing ever happened. To go from 110 pounds and losing weight rapidly to weighing 142 pounds all within a matter of months is awesome. To go from having little to no strength to having renewed strength and greater vitality than I had before is astounding. I too was like one who dreamed. I no longer had a vision of healing, I was healed. I no longer had a dream of being healing, I was healed.

Friends my body responded to the Word of God. My body responded to the prayers. My body responded to the confessions I spoke. My body responded to faith in God. The Bible said in Mark 11:22-23, "Jesus told his disciples,

Have faith in God...I tell you with certainty, if anyone says to this mountain, Be lifted up and be cast into the sea, if he does not doubt in his heart but believes that what he says will happen, it will be done for him."

I pray that you will take these same principles and apply them to your life. Speak to your mountain. My prayer is that you will be healed, in your mind, body, soul, and spirit in Jesus' name.

Reflections

Questions

1. My mountain was cancer. What is yours?

2. According to Matthew 11:22-23, what are you speaking towards your mountain?

3. Has God ever answered your prayer beyond your wildest dream?

Reflections

Reflections

A FINAL NOTE

It is recommended that a preventive colonoscopy screening is done beginning at age 45. And even sooner if there is a personal history or family history of colon cancer.

Please listen to your body. Consult with your doctor and have regular exams and screenings.

The natural and supernatural can work together to bring healing to your body.

For more information on colon cancer visit cancer.org

Love,

Dr. Andrea Hill

www.ingramcontent.com/pod-product-compliance
Lightning Source LLC
Chambersburg PA
CBHW030838090426
42737CB00009B/1017